THE ROAD TO RETIREMENT

A Guaranteed-Income Blueprint
for Business Owners Who Want to Retire Rich

THE ROAD TO RETIREMENT

A Guaranteed-Income Blueprint for Business Owners Who Want to Retire Rich

VIKAS ARORA

Available on amazonkindle

Worldwide Published by

Pendown Press

PREMIUM BUSINESS PUBLISHER

PENDOWN PRESS LLP
An ISO 9001 & ISO 14001 Certified Co.,
Regd. Office: 3767A, Kanhaiya Nagar,
Tri Nagar, Delhi-110035
Ph.: 8130886000, 9650072927
E-mail: info@pendownpress.com
Branch Office: 1A/2A, 20, Hari Sadan, Ansari Road,
Daryaganj, New Delhi-110002
Ph.: 011-45794768
Website: PendownPress.com

Edition: 2026
Price: ₹ 399
ISBN: 978-93-7217-965-1

Layout and Cover Designed by Pendown Graphics Team

Table of Content

Acknowledgment i

Prologue: The Journey to Your Future, Work-Free Adventures iii

Preface: Your Future Deserves a Plan, Not a Gamble v

Chapter 1	Introduction to Retirement Planning	1
Chapter 2	Embracing the Second Innings The Joy of a Work-Free Retirement	7
Chapter 3	The Power of the Purse Financial Independence and Dignity in Old Age	13
Chapter 4	Your Money, Your Strength Building a Solid Financial Foundation for Retirement	17
Chapter 5	A Life of Independence No Dependence on Children for Financial Support	23
Chapter 6	The Essential Expenses How to Cover them with a Retirement Plan	29
Chapter 7	The Principles of Effective Retirement Planning	35
Chapter 8	Retirement Savings and Investment Options	39
Chapter 9	Healthcare and Retirement	45

Chapter 10 Estate Planning and Legacy 51

Chapter 11 Stepping into Tomorrow
The Confidence of a Well-Planned
Retirement 55

Bonus Chapter

New Age Retirement Strategies for a Changing India 57

DEDICATION

This book is lovingly dedicated to my parents,
Sh. J R Arora and (Late) Smt. Usha Arora.

Their blessings, understanding, support, and above all, love, have been the driving force behind the completion of this work.

Their constant encouragement has made this journey possible and meaningful.

Acknowledgements

I extend my heartfelt gratitude to the numerous individuals who have played a pivotal role in bringing this book to fruition. Their unwavering support, insightful discussions, constructive feedback, and assistance in editing, proofreading, and design have been invaluable to this project's success.

Foremost, I express my deepest appreciation to my parents, whose constant love and guidance have been an unwavering source of strength throughout this endeavour. They are my ultimate role models, and I am profoundly grateful for their encouragement.

I would like to extend special thanks to my mentors,

1. **Sh. R. Gopinath**, M/s Gopast Centre for Learning Pvt. Ltd., Chennai.
2. Mr. Rahul Jain (India's Leading Business Coach)
3. Mr. Akshar Yadav (Creator of the Get Overbooked framework and No.1 Marketing and life coach)

Their profound teachings on various concepts have been instrumental in helping me reach the milestones of this journey. I am humbled by their blessings and eager to continue learning from them.

My heartfelt thanks go to my loving and supportive wife, Priyal, and my two wonderful children, Daksh and Saanvi. Their unyielding encouragement and inspiration have been an anchor in my pursuit of this project.

Lastly, I sincerely apologise to all those who have been part of my 26-year journey and whose names might have inadvertently been omitted in this acknowledgment. Your contributions have been deeply valued and appreciated.

Thank you all for being an integral part of this remarkable journey.

PROLOGUE

The Journey to Your Future, Work-Free Adventures

> *"Retirement is when you stop living at work and start working at living."*
> ***– Unknown***

You know that cosy feeling when you settle into your favourite chair, a warm drink in hand, with zero work emails to check?

That's a snippet of what retirement feels like.

But **to truly enjoy those endless free days, you need a plan.**

Life's a whirlwind, right? You're always chasing something - a promotion, a new project, or that dream home. Yet, amidst this chase, there's another future waiting: a time when the hustle slows down, and the simple joys take centre stage.

That future is retirement, and it's closer than it seems.

In this book, you and I are going on a journey. Together, we'll unlock the secrets to making your post-working years the best they can be.

We'll hear tales of and learn lessons from people just like you, who've stepped into their golden years.

Some had it all planned out, enjoying their free time without counting pennies.

Others?

Well, they stumbled a bit, learning lessons the hard way.

Their stories will be our roadmap, teaching us what to embrace and what pitfalls to avoid.

Every chapter here is a tool.

From understanding how to save without cutting out life's little treats, to making sure you've got a safety net for those just-in-case moments.

- Maybe you're someone who's been clocking in 9-to-5 for years.
- Or perhaps you're an entrepreneur, managing your business empire.

Whoever you are, this guide's got your back.

Beyond the money talk, we'll also chat about the emotional side of things. Because leaving the work world isn't just about bank balances, it's a new life chapter.

- How do we adjust?
- How do we find new passions?

Don't worry; we've got that covered, too.

So, if you've ever dreamt of long, lazy days reading by the beach, taking impromptu trips, indulging in hobbies, or simply spending quality time with loved ones without any work stress, you're in the right place.

Grab a comfy spot and your favourite beverage. It's time to plan for those epic, work-free adventures ahead. Let's dive in!

PREFACE

Your Future Deserves a Plan, Not a Gamble

"Your future is created by what you do today, not tomorrow."
– Robert Kiyosaki

As witnessed in the prologue above, the idea of retirement often conjures up images of leisurely days, free from the demands of a daily work routine. But the transition from a structured career to a life of freedom requires careful planning and understanding, perhaps more than most of us realize.

"The Road to Retirement: Navigating Your Way to Financial Independence" was born out of a desire to guide individuals from all walks of life in crafting a fulfilling and secure retirement. It's not just about numbers, investments, or financial strategies; it's about embracing a new phase of life with excitement, dignity, and confidence.

The Why Behind This Book?

Retirement planning is no longer a concern only for the elite or the financial experts. In today's rapidly changing economic environment, where social security nets might not be enough, and traditional pension plans are dwindling, every individual needs to take charge of their financial future.

This book is not a theoretical or technical manual filled with financial jargon.

Instead, it's a friendly guide written for laymen:

- Offering practical advice,
- Real-life examples,
- And actionable steps.

Whether you are:

- A young adult starting your career,
- A mid-career professional evaluating your savings,
- Or someone approaching retirement

"The Road to Retirement" is tailored to help you.

What's Inside?

You'll find chapters dedicated to different facets of retirement planning, from building a solid financial foundation to navigating the emotional aspects of retiring. Special emphasis is given to the joy of financial independence, dignity in old age, healthcare considerations, estate planning, and even common mistakes to avoid.

- There are exercises, checklists, and case studies to engage you in your journey.
- The book encourages reflection and application, not just reading and forgetting.

In between the pages, you'll discover:

- The power and magic of compound interest, and how it can be your ally.

- Methods to calculate the exact financial corpus you'd need to retire comfortably.
- The significance of reframing your budgeting mindset to prioritize savings.
- Answers to the most frequently asked questions about retirement, demystifying complex concepts in layman's terms.
- And much more.

Retirement planning is a personal and unique journey.

What works for one person may not suit another. This book recognizes that individuality and aims to equip you with the tools and understanding to carve out your path.

Whether you're in your 20s or your 60s, it's never too early or too late to think about retirement.

This book is your compass, pointing you towards a future where financial worries don't cloud your sunset years.

So, Who Should Read This Book

- **Aspiring Retirees:** If you're nearing retirement and want to enter this new phase with confidence, this book will guide you through every essential step.
- **Early Career Professionals:** Learn why starting early matters. Build smart saving and investing habits that secure your future from day one.
- **Mid-Career Professionals:** Reassess your financial goals, diversify wisely, and realign your strategy as retirement draws closer.
- **Financial Advisors:** Gain practical insights, updated strategies, and real-world examples to better guide your clients.
- **Individuals with Dependents:** Plan a secure future for your family while ensuring your own financial independence.

- **Health-Conscious Individuals:** Understand how to prepare for rising healthcare costs and protect your retirement corpus.
- **Parents & Grandparents:** Discover how to leave a meaningful legacy without compromising your own needs.
- **People Seeking Financial Independence:** If freedom from financial dependence is your goal, this book shows you the way.
- **Those Interested in Psychology:** Explore the emotional and mental shifts that come with retiring and how to embrace them.
- **Case Study Enthusiasts:** Enjoy relatable real-life stories and learn from others who've successfully planned their retirement.

How to Use This Book

This book is designed as a step-by-step companion to help you plan, prepare, and enjoy a financially independent retirement.

Here's how to get the most from it:

1. **Start with the Basics**

   Chapter 1: Understand why retirement planning matters and how it shapes your future.

2. **Explore Retirement Perspectives**

   Chapters 2 - 3: Discover the joy of financial freedom and dignity in your second innings.

   Chapters 4 - 5: Learn how savings, investments, and self-reliance build long-term strength.

3. **Plan and Implement Strategies**

   Chapters 6 - 7: Create your retirement blueprint by identifying key expenses and principles.

   Chapter 8: Explore saving and investment options to build a balanced portfolio.

Chapter 9: Integrate healthcare into your plan and prepare for medical costs.

4. **Learn from Experience**

   Chapter 11: Get inspired by real-life retirement success stories.

   Chapter 12: Avoid common planning mistakes and stay on track.

5. **Manage the Emotional and Legacy Aspects**

   Chapter 10: Learn how to plan your legacy with confidence.

   Chapter 13: Navigate the emotional transition to a fulfilling retired life.

6. **Use the Tools Provided**

   Chapter 14: Apply the Retirement Checklist to measure your readiness.

   Exercises and Examples: Complete hands-on tasks to make learning practical.

   Family Discussions: Share insights with loved ones to build mutual understanding.

In Short

This book is more than a guide; it's your lifelong partner on the journey to a secure, independent, and joyful retirement.

Who Am I, and Why You Should Take My Advice

If you're wondering why you should trust me to talk about retirement planning, let me start by saying this: I've lived and breathed it for more than two decades.

Since **1999**, I've had the privilege of **helping over 1,600 families plan their financial futures,** guiding them towards true independence and peace of mind. Together, we've settled **maturity**

claims worth 93.75 crore and **life claims worth 10.20 crore,** but more importantly, we've built lasting confidence in the power of planning ahead.

I began my journey after graduating from **Delhi University**, and along the way, earned professional certifications from the **National Institute of Securities Market (NISM)** and the **Business Mastery Program, BCI Lead by India's leading Business Coach, Mr. Rahul Jain**. I hold both the **Foundation** and **Master Level Certifications in Applied Financial Planning from Gopast Centre for Learning**, which have strengthened my practical experience with solid financial science.-

I have also qualified for the Award in Financial Planning from the Chartered Insurance Institute, London. In addition, I have graduated from the Get Overbooked Academy under the guidance of India's No. 1 Marketing Guru and mentor, Mr. Akshar Yadav.

Over the years, I've been honoured with some of the highest industry recognitions, **qualified MDRT (1 time)**, **Court of the Table (3 Times)**, and **Top of the Table (2 Times),** achievements that reflect my commitment to excellence and ethics. My journey has also taken me to **London, Sydney, Dubai, Switzerland, Georgia, Singapore, and Moscow** as part of international conventions with **Tata AIA, Tata AIG**, & **Niva Bupa Health Insurance**

Today, I lead a passionate team of 20 professionals from our offices in **Netaji Subhash Place, Pitampura**, and **Keshav Puram**, where our shared goal is simple: **to help people gain clarity, confidence, and control over their financial lives.**

This book is a reflection of everything I've learned from real people and real stories. My hope is that it gives you not just financial knowledge, but the belief that your second innings can be truly your best.

Retirement planning may seem daunting, but it's an empowering process. Taking control of your financial future, understanding your options, and making informed decisions can bring peace of mind and open doors to new possibilities.

I invite you to embark on this exciting journey through "The Road to Retirement." May it enlighten, empower, and inspire you as you navigate your way to a fulfilling and financially independent retirement.

Happy reading and an even happier retirement!

Vikas Arora

CHAPTER 1

INTRODUCTION TO RETIREMENT PLANNING

"The goal of retirement is to live life on your own terms, not on life's uncertainties."
– Vikas Arora

The Concept of Retirement Planning

Retirement planning is an essential financial strategy that aims to ensure a comfortable life after your regular professional income stops.

It involves:

- Understanding your retirement income goals
- Assessing your current financial situation
- And formulating an action plan to meet those goals

The objective is to guarantee your financial independence and help you maintain the lifestyle you desire in your golden years.

A Historical Perspective of Retirement and Retirement Planning

Historically, the concept of retirement was virtually nonexistent. Prior to the 19th century, most people worked until their physical abilities declined, often until their death.

In Germany, under Otto von Bismarck, the first systematic old-age pension plan was introduced in 1889. This plan was initiated as a social insurance program for the elderly, responding to societal changes due to the Industrial Revolution.

The concept of retirement, and consequently retirement planning, in India took shape post the colonial rule. The British established a pension system for civil servants, and post-independence, the government took measures to widen the social security coverage.

However, the need for personal retirement planning in India has been emphasized only in recent years due to various social and economic shifts.

Why is Retirement Planning Essential?

The reasons are twofold.

1. **Firstly,** people are now leading longer, healthier lives, requiring planning for more years of post-retirement living expenses. As of 2021, the World Health Organization (WHO) estimated the global average life expectancy to be 73.3 years, necessitating a substantial retirement corpus.
2. **Secondly,** rapid changes in the cultural fabric of India have brought new challenges. The traditional reliance on children to support parents in their old age is declining, and with the

emergence of nuclear families, planning for a self-sufficient retirement is of the essence.

Factors Influencing Retirement Planning

Retirement planning demands an understanding of factors such as:

- **Inflation** [Inflation erodes the purchasing power of money over time. Therefore, your retirement corpus should be substantial enough to account for this decrease in purchasing power, ensuring your passive income maintains your desired lifestyle.]
- **Healthcare costs** [Healthcare costs, often underestimated, can significantly drain retirement savings. As we age, healthcare needs increase and therefore should be factored into retirement planning.]
- **Lifestyle aspirations** [retirement should not be viewed merely as the cessation of active income, but as a phase to pursue hobbies, travel, and spend quality time with loved ones. Therefore, one's lifestyle aspirations should be taken into account while planning for retirement.]

All these costs, when calculated and considered at the beginning of your career, allow for an extended accumulation period, making them more manageable to achieve at your desired level by the time you retire.

Furthermore,

The Process of Retirement Planning

The process of retirement planning begins with:

- Understanding one's income and expenses,
- Followed by setting retirement goals.

The subsequent steps involve:

- Determining the retirement corpus needed
- Planning the investments accordingly,
- And finally, executing the plan.

Each step is interconnected and crucial for the successful generation of a sufficient passive income during retirement years.

The importance of starting early can't be overstressed, as starting early allows compounding to work its magic, making it easier to accumulate a substantial corpus.

For retirement planning to be successful, it must be flexible, adjusting to the changes in one's life.

Major life events such as marriage, childbirth, and changes in career or income levels might necessitate a revisit of the retirement plan. It's essential to reassess and realign the retirement plan with these changes, ensuring it remains robust and capable of achieving the desired passive income.

Peace of Mind through Retirement Planning

A well-laid retirement plan provides more than just financial security; it gives peace of mind. It relieves the anxiety about the future and provides a safety net for any unforeseen circumstances. It ensures that you are prepared for life's eventualities and allows you to live your retirement years on your terms.

Retirement Planning and Financial Education

Successful retirement planning is impossible to achieve without financial education. It plays a vital role in the process.

It equips individuals with:

- **The knowledge** to make informed decisions about their investments,

- **Understand the risks** associated with various financial products,
- **And choose t**he ones that best suit their retirement goals and risk tolerance.

The Crucial Role of Financial Advisors in Retirement Planning

Financial advisors can be valuable allies in the retirement planning process.

They can provide:

- Expert advice,
- Offer personalized retirement plans,
- And help monitor and adjust the plan as needed.

Their expertise in financial matters can be a significant asset in making sound investment decisions and navigating the complexities of retirement planning.

Retirement Planning for Women

Retirement planning for women deserves special mention. Women generally live longer than men and may have different career trajectories due to responsibilities like childcare and eldercare. These factors must be taken into account in retirement planning, making sure that women can maintain their lifestyle and financial independence throughout their retirement years.

Retirement Planning and Social Security

While personal retirement planning is critical, it's also important to understand the role of social security benefits in your retirement plan. These benefits, while not sufficient to rely on solely, can provide a stable income source during retirement and act as a safety net.

Lastly, while retirement planning may seem daunting, remember that it's a gradual process. It's about making consistent efforts and disciplined investment decisions.

- A slow and steady approach, coupled with patience and regular monitoring, is the key to building a substantial retirement corpus.

With careful planning and execution, you can ensure that your retirement years are as fulfilling and financially secure as your working years, offering you the freedom to enjoy the fruits of your lifelong labor.

CHAPTER 2

EMBRACING THE SECOND INNINGS
THE JOY OF A WORK-FREE RETIREMENT

"In retirement, every day is yours: your time, your pace, your life. Plan well, retire free, live fully."
– Vikas Arora

Be Work-Free, not Income-Free

Retirement, often referred to as the second innings of life, should ideally be a period of relaxation, personal fulfilment, and enjoyment. However, to truly experience the joys of this stage, one needs to have financial stability and independence. **A well-devised retirement strategy can ensure a steady stream of income even when you are not working.**

Knowing you are financially secure allows you to focus on aspects of life that are not dominated by work pressures. It's a period when no more struggling for survival is required. Your past efforts and smart financial planning pave the way for a smooth, worry-free existence.

Work-Free Doesn't Mean Idle

When we discuss work-free retirement, we are talking about an era of life liberated from the compulsion to earn. This doesn't mean that one can't work or pursue a hobby that might bring in income.

The difference is that post-retirement, work becomes a matter of choice rather than necessity.

Many individuals find joy in turning their hobbies into businesses or consulting in their field of expertise at their own pace. Yet, they do so for personal satisfaction, staying active, keeping their minds sharp, or contributing to society rather than merely for monetary needs.

One of the greatest benefits of a work-free retirement is the freedom to spend your time as you wish.

- Always wanted to travel and explore different cultures? Now is the time.
- Have a knack for gardening but never had the time to invest? You can now create your dream garden.
- Wished to learn a musical instrument or a new language? There's no better time than retirement to indulge in these passions.

With financial independence, you don't need to compromise on your wishes. You have the liberty to follow your desires and invest your time in activities that make you happy.

Mrs. Rajni Kapoor: A Kathak Maestro at 62

Mrs. Kapoor, a retired bank officer from Mumbai, had a lifelong desire to learn Kathak, an Indian classical dance form; however, due to work and home commitments, she never could find the time or energy.

Post-retirement, she not only had the time, **but her well-planned retirement strategy also allowed her to afford to enroll in a reputed Kathak school after retirement.**

She not only learned the art form and fulfilled her life-long wish, but **also performs at local events, earning accolades and appreciations.**

A work-free retirement also allows you to contribute to society and engage with your community in ways you couldn't before.

- Volunteering for a cause you care about
- Mentoring younger generations
- Getting involved in local governance

These are some ways you can use your skills and experience to make a difference.

Retirement provides a golden opportunity to give back to the community in meaningful ways.

Mr. Prakash Lighting Up & Enriching the Community Through Service

Mr. Prakash, a retired school teacher from Delhi, **had always dreamt of starting a small library in his locality post-retirement.**

Thanks to his timely investments in a mix of fixed deposits, PPF, and mutual funds, he was able to realize his dream.

Today, he runs a small but flourishing library, earning admiration and respect from his community.

Healthy Living in Retirement

Another crucial aspect of this phase is to maintain a healthy lifestyle. You have the time to focus on your physical well-being. Regular exercise, healthy eating, and regular medical check-ups become easier to manage in retirement, contributing to better health and longevity.

Retirement is not only a time for financial freedom but also for investing in your health, which can pay dividends in terms of improved quality of life and increased lifespan.

Cultivating Relationships in Retirement

Retirement can also be a time for deepening relationships and spending quality time with loved ones. The hustle and bustle of professional life often leaves little time for family and friends. However, in retirement, you can enjoy moments of togetherness, creating lasting memories. It is a unique time that allows you to strengthen your relationships, build new connections, and create a support system that can be incredibly valuable.

The Joy of Learning and Intellectual & Spiritual Growth

Many individuals utilize their retirement years to continue their intellectual growth. Whether it's finally having the time to read the classics, enrolling in an online course, or even going back to school, retirement can be a period of intense learning and exploration.

For some, retirement offers an opportunity for introspection and spiritual growth. This stage of life can provide the time and space to delve deeper into your spiritual beliefs, practice mindfulness, or explore different philosophies. This kind of personal growth can bring inner peace, happiness, and a sense of fulfilment that complements the financial stability achieved through effective retirement planning.

Planning for a Fulfilling Retirement

A work-free retirement can be the most fulfilling and satisfying phase of life. It offers unlimited opportunities to explore new interests, pursue passions, deepen relationships, and contribute to society. It provides the freedom to live life on your terms, unbound by monetary concerns.

However, the key to enjoying this freedom lies in an effective retirement strategy, which eliminates the need for struggling for survival or compromising on wishes. It's important to plan early and make informed decisions. Financial independence does not come overnight; it is the result of years of diligent saving, smart investing, and prudent spending. Plan wisely, live freely, and make your second innings truly remarkable.

CHAPTER 3

THE POWER OF THE PURSE

FINANCIAL INDEPENDENCE AND DIGNITY IN OLD AGE

"Financial Independence is the Foundation of a Self-Driven & Empowered Life."
– Vikas Arora

Financial independence in retirement is not just about being able to meet daily needs and occasional luxuries. It's about dignity, self-respect, and the power to make personal choices.

The sense of self-worth that comes from managing your own finances, without relying on anyone else, cannot be understated.

It gives one the power to decide the course of their life, providing the flexibility to choose where to live, how to live, and what activities to engage in.

Whether it's buying a retirement home in a peaceful locale, traveling to a long-desired destination, or picking up a new hobby, financial independence ensures that you're in control.

- Importantly, financial independence also reinforces self-esteem and dignity.

- It allows you to uphold your standard of living and preserve your self-respect.
- With your own financial resources, you're not obligated to anyone, and you don't need to compromise on your wants or needs.
- You can afford the best possible healthcare, engage in recreational activities,
- And live a fulfilling life that is not confined by financial constraints.

Effective Retirement Planning for Financial Independence

Financial independence at an old age is a result of prudent retirement planning.

Savings and investments made during the working years compound over time to build a significant corpus that can be relied upon post-retirement.

Retirement strategies such as investing in:

- Life insurance,
- Mutual funds,
- PPF,
- And annuity schemes

can ensure a steady income flow in the later years of life.

Exploring New Avenues: The Courage to Take Risks

Financial independence gives you the courage to take risks and try new things. Be it starting a small business, investing in a new venture, or experimenting with a new hobby, you have the financial security to take chances.

These risks can lead to exciting new opportunities, rewarding experiences, and even new income streams.

Passing on Wisdom and Leaving a Legacy

Financial independence in retirement allows you **to share your life lessons with younger generations,** teaching them the value of saving, investing, and planning ahead, **as you are the perfect example of embodying and living what you preach. This guidance helps them build strong financial habits early in life.**

It also enables you to leave a meaningful legacy. Whether through an inheritance, property, or contributions to causes you care about, you can create something that lasts beyond your lifetime. This ability to support and shape the future brings deep fulfilment and purpose.

Maintaining Self-Identity: Independence as a Key Aspect

In an era where self-identity is increasingly important, financial independence in retirement reinforces your sense of self. It allows you to continue being the person you've always been, without the fear of becoming dependent or a burden. This independence reinforces your identity and instills a sense of confidence that contributes to a healthier and happier life.

The Iyers Living Life on Their Own Terms as Always

Mrs. and Mr. Iyer, a retired couple from Chennai, are a classic example of how to maintain dignity in old age through financial independence.

They started planning for their retirement in their early 30s by investing in PPF, mutual funds, and a life insurance annuity plan.

Today, they live in their own house, manage their expenses comfortably, and even afford occasional luxuries like foreign vacations.

In conclusion, financial independence in old age is vital for maintaining dignity and self-respect. It allows you to live your life as per your wishes, without having to rely on anyone else for your financial needs. This independence does not come easily but is the result of diligent planning, disciplined saving, and prudent investing during the working years. Remember, the power of the purse in old age is not just about wealth; it's about maintaining your dignity, preserving your self-respect, and living a fulfilling and comfortable life.

CHAPTER 4

YOUR MONEY, YOUR STRENGTH

BUILDING A SOLID FINANCIAL FOUNDATION FOR RETIREMENT

> *"The money you save & invest today becomes the freedom you live with tomorrow."*
> ***– Vikas Arora***

The key to a peaceful and fulfilling retirement lies in having a robust financial foundation that allows you to live life on your terms. Building your savings and making smart investments over your working years can strengthen your position during retirement and provide a sense of empowerment and security.

The practice of saving is a fundamental habit to build financial stability.

- Consistent savings over the years act as a cornerstone for your retirement corpus.
- They provide a financial safety net that can help navigate unexpected situations such as health emergencies or sudden lifestyle changes.

Savings also contribute to maintaining your standard of living post-retirement. It allows you to be financially independent, preserving your self-respect and dignity by letting you make your own financial decisions.

Investments: Amplifying Wealth Through Calculated Risks

While savings set the base, it's through investments that your wealth can grow and yield fruitful returns. Wise and diversified investments during your working years can result in a steady income stream in your retirement years, giving you financial security and independence.

Investments can take various forms, like:

- Equities,
- Bonds,
- Mutual funds,
- Real estate
- Retirement schemes like PPF
- And life insurance endowment policies.

The investment choices you make during your working years can dictate the kind of lifestyle you can afford during retirement.

Crafting an Effective Investment Strategy: Balancing Risk and Reward

Investing comes with its own set of risks and rewards.

- High-risk investments might yield higher returns, but they also carry a greater risk of losses.
- As you near retirement, it might be advisable to shift towards lower-risk investments to preserve your hard-earned corpus.
- Diversification, i.e., spreading your investments across various asset classes, can help strike a balance between risk and reward.
- It's all about creating a portfolio that fits your risk tolerance and retirement goals.

The Crucial Role of a Financial Advisor in Retirement Planning

Getting professional help can prove extremely advantageous while planning for retirement.

A competent financial advisor can help you:

- Understand your financial standing,
- Align your investments with your retirement goals
- Help you navigate through complex financial decisions
- Assist you in crafting an effective investment strategy, considering your risk appetite and long-term objectives.

Financial planning for retirement is not a one-time exercise but a continuous process.

It requires revisiting and adjusting your financial plan according to changing life stages, market fluctuations, and your evolving financial goals.

Regular monitoring and timely adjustments ensure that your retirement corpus is on track and is resilient to unexpected financial shocks.

Building a solid financial foundation for retirement also involves estate planning.

It's about deciding how you want your assets to be distributed after your demise. A well-structured estate plan can help minimize taxes, protect your assets, and ensure that your loved ones are taken care of. It's an essential part of retirement planning that provides peace of mind and financial security to your family.

Fun Facts: Lessons from Bollywood

Highlighting the Importance of Financial Independence

Indian cinema, or Bollywood, often reflects societal norms and lessons, including the importance of financial independence during retirement.

Let's revisit a few popular movie examples that effectively highlight these concepts:

"Baghban"

A Stark Reminder of the Consequences of Neglecting Retirement Planning

The movie "Baghban" tells the story of a couple who, due to insufficient savings and also their overgenerosity that their children take advantage of, have to depend on their children in their old age, losing their dignity in the process.

It underscores the importance of personal savings and treating them as sacred, as well as the power they hold in preserving one's self-respect during the twilight years.

"102 Not Out"

Celebrating the Joy of Financial Independence in Old Age

In contrast to "Baghban," "102 Not Out" illustrates a positive perspective on old age. Amitabh Bachchan's character lives an independent, content life at 102, demonstrating the freedom and dignity that come with financial independence.

- Building a strong financial foundation for retirement doesn't happen overnight.
- It's a journey that involves consistent savings, thoughtful investments, and prudent financial decisions over the years.
- By maintaining financial discipline during your working years, you can strengthen your financial position for your golden years, providing a sense of security and empowerment.

The stories and lessons from Bollywood reiterate these facts, showing that retirement can be a time of fulfillment and peace when you have your finances in order.

After all, in retirement, your money truly becomes your strength.

CHAPTER 5

A LIFE OF INDEPENDENCE
NO DEPENDENCE ON CHILDREN FOR FINANCIAL SUPPORT

> *"Retirement becomes freedom when your needs are met by your planning, not your children's sacrifices."*
> ***– Vikas Arora***

The desire for financial independence during retirement is a common and cherished goal. The modern retiree aspires to be self-reliant. This autonomy allows individuals to live with dignity, chase their personal hobbies and interests, and completely removes the necessity to depend on children or others for financial support. This chapter delves deep into the value of such independence and how systematic retirement planning facilitates this goal.

Preparing for a Confident & Independent Retirement

Financial independence in retirement is the outcome of clear goals, steady savings, and thoughtful decisions taken throughout one's working life.

Retirement planning begins with:

- Understanding what your future expenses will look like
- Knowing the sources of income you will rely on

- And preparing for essential needs such as healthcare and day-to-day living.

When done early, planning becomes a powerful shield against the biggest fears of old age: rising medical costs, the possibility of outliving one's savings, and the risk of becoming dependent on children.

Building Stability: The Power of Endowment Plans and Annuities

Among the many ways to build a strong financial foundation, **life insurance endowment plans and annuity schemes offer some of the most dependable support.**

- Endowment plans encourage systematic savings and create a large, guaranteed corpus at maturity.
- When this corpus is converted into an annuity, it becomes a steady lifelong income. The combination creates safety, predictability, and peace of mind.

Mr Kartik Sharma's Early Start Helps His Later Life Bloom

Mr Sharma, a bank manager, made a simple yet powerful choice **at the age of 30 by beginning an endowment plan.**

Over the years, he paid his premiums regularly.

When the policy matured, **he used the accumulated amount to purchase an annuity that now pays him a fixed income every month.**

Today, he enjoys complete financial independence, covers his healthcare comfortably, and never has to worry about asking his children for support.

His story shows how early decisions create lifelong stability.

The Couple Who Started Late: A Life of Regrets

In contrast to Mr. Sharma, on the other side of the spectrum were Mrs and Mr Rao, **who only began thinking about retirement in their mid-50s.**

As a result of the delayed initiative, their savings were limited, and a sudden medical emergency consumed most of it.

They now depend on their son for expenses, which has created **guilt for them and stress for him.**

Their story highlights what many retirees discover too late: planning early avoids hardship later.

Key Insights to Ensure an Empowered Retirement

1. **Healthcare Realities: Preparing for the Biggest Expense**

   One of the highest costs in old age is healthcare. As medical needs increase, savings can shrink rapidly. A dedicated healthcare fund ensures that hospital bills do not force you to compromise on your well-being or depend on your children during emergencies. It also helps you afford quality care without financial fear.

2. **Ensuring Your Money Lasts: The Fear of Outliving Savings**

   Nearly every retiree worries that their money may run out before they do. This fear is real and often justified. But it can be managed through long-term planning, disciplined saving, and choosing financial products like annuities that promise guaranteed income for life. A well-structured plan ensures that you remain confident and financially comfortable throughout your retirement.

3. **Living Smart: Downsizing and Simpler Choices**

   Some people strengthen their retirement security by simplifying their lifestyle. Downsizing to a smaller home, reducing unnecessary expenses, or choosing a slower, more relaxed pace of life can help savings stretch much longer. These changes are not sacrifices but practical adjustments that bring comfort and peace.

4. **Staying Informed: Lifelong Learning for Financial Confidence**

   Understanding financial tools and keeping yourself updated with basic financial knowledge helps you make informed decisions. Even simple awareness of interest rates, investment options, or insurance products can prevent costly mistakes and support long-term independence.

5. **The Emotional Side: Avoiding Dependence and Regret**

   Dependence on children, though common, often brings emotional strain. Many parents feel guilty using resources their children need for their own families and goals. This guilt can silently affect self-worth. Regret also troubles those who did not plan early enough. Many realise later that they underestimated expenses or assumed that their children would automatically support them. Planning well ensures dignity, confidence, and freedom.

6. **Finding Purpose: Staying Active in Retirement**

   Many retirees miss the work routines that once gave them purpose. But financial independence allows them to pursue hobbies, learn something new, travel, or even take up part-time work by choice rather than need. When money does not limit possibilities, retirement becomes a phase of renewal and exploration.

7. **Leaving a Legacy: Planning Beyond Yourself**

   Thoughtful retirement planning not only secures your own life but also allows you to leave a legacy for your children or for causes you care about. Whether it is property, investments, or charitable contributions, wealth passed on with intention can support the next generation meaningfully.

Kavita's Dilemma: Supporting Two Generations

Kavita, a 42-year-old single mother, is **supporting her school-going son and her retired parents.**

With no retirement fund of their own, **her parents rely entirely on her income. This leaves Kavita little room to save for her son's education or her own future.**

Her struggle shows **how parents' lack of planning can unintentionally burden the next generation at the hardest stage of their lives.**

The ultimate purpose of retirement planning is freedom: the freedom to live with dignity, to make your own choices, and to stay independent without burdening your children.

When you invest time, money, and discipline into building your retirement future, you give yourself comfort in your later years and give your children peace of mind.

Retirement becomes not only a phase of dependence but a stage of strength, confidence, and well-deserved joy.

CHAPTER 6

THE ESSENTIAL EXPENSES
HOW TO COVER THEM WITH A RETIREMENT PLAN

"A peaceful retirement is not bought with wealth, but with the wisdom to plan for every essential need before the need arises."
– Vikas Arora

The transition to retirement ushers in a new financial era in one's life. The regular income flow from work ceases, leaving the management of daily expenses to the savings and investments accumulated throughout the working years. These expenses, known as 'essential expenses', include everything necessary for comfortable living - from housing and utilities to food, healthcare, and transportation.

Identifying Essential Expenses: What Constitutes Them?

Accurate identification and estimation of essential expenses are vital as they form the foundation of your retirement budget.

The cost of living, including:

- Rent or property maintenance,
- Utility bills,

- Groceries,
- Clothing,
- Transportation, etc.

are consistent expenses.

- Healthcare costs, often underestimated, gain increasing significance as we age.
- Other considerations might include insurance premiums, taxes, and potential debts.

The Expense - Income Matching Strategy: Sizing Up Financial Needs

One way to plan for retirement is by matching certain income streams with certain expenses. This can help ensure that you have a reliable source of income to cover each of your basic needs. This strategy works well for expenses that are predictable and regular. For example, rental income from a property investment could be used to cover housing and utility costs, while returns from a fixed deposit could be dedicated to food and transportation costs.

One critical factor to consider while planning for retirement expenses is inflation.

The cost of living tends to rise over time, eroding the purchasing power of your savings.

Inflation: The Silent Killer

For instance, if you require 1 lakh per month for your family's expenses today, considering an average inflation rate of 6%, you will need approximately 4 lakhs per month to maintain the same standard of living 20 years from now.

Financial Instruments for Retirement: Understanding The Spectrum

Once you've estimated your essential expenses, taking into account future inflation, the next step is to identify how to cover these expenses during retirement.

This involves understanding the range of financial instruments available, each of which offers different benefits and is suitable for different goals.

1. **Mutual Funds, Stocks, and Bonds: Growing Your Wealth**

   Investments in mutual funds, stocks, and bonds aim to grow your wealth over time. They offer returns that can potentially outpace inflation, making them a viable option for wealth accumulation. Systematic withdrawal from these investments can provide a regular income stream to meet ongoing expenses.

2. **Fixed Deposits and PPF: The Reliability of Fixed Returns**

   Investments like Fixed Deposits and Public Provident Fund (PPF) offer stable returns, thereby providing a dependable source of income during retirement. Given their low-risk nature, these instruments are well-suited for covering regular, predictable expenses.

3. **Real Estate: Rent and Capital Appreciation**

   Real estate investments can serve as a dual-purpose tool in your retirement plan. They can generate rental income to supplement your regular cash flow, and as the property appreciates, it becomes a valuable asset that can be liquidated in later years for significant lump-sum amounts, useful for unexpected costs or enhanced lifestyle expenses.

4. **Life Insurance and Annuity Schemes:**

   A Stable Income Stream

   Life insurance endowment plans and annuity schemes provide a guaranteed income stream during retirement, ensuring financial security and peace of mind. Given their stability and predictability, they are ideal for meeting essential expenses.

5. **Health Insurance: A Shield Against Medical Expenses**

   Health insurance plays a pivotal role in managing healthcare costs. With advancing age and associated health risks, medical expenses can escalate rapidly. A robust health insurance policy can cover these costs, safeguarding your retirement corpus from premature depletion due to unexpected health issues.

Key Insights to Keep in Mind While Choosing Your Instruments

The Critical Role of Diversification: Spreading Your Eggs

In financial parlance, 'diversification' is a mantra often preached and practiced. It pertains to the method of spreading investments across a variety of financial instruments, thereby reducing exposure to any single asset or risk. The underlying principle is simple, but powerful: "Do not put all your eggs in one basket."

A well-rounded retirement plan diversifies investments across various financial instruments. Diversification ensures that while some investments focus on wealth growth, others provide steady, reliable income. This strategy reduces overall risk and provides multiple income streams to cater to different expenses.

The Buffer Strategy: Anticipating Unexpected Costs

Even with meticulous planning, unexpected expenses can arise during retirement, necessitating an additional financial buffer. This could be a contingency fund set aside specifically to meet unexpected costs, or the inclusion of flexible financial instruments within your portfolio that allow early withdrawal or loans.

Adjusting Your Retirement Plan: Staying Dynamic

Retirement planning isn't a one-off task. As you progress closer to your retirement years, the plan needs periodic review and adjustments to align with changes in lifestyle, health, market conditions, and financial goals. This flexibility in your retirement plan helps ensure that it remains effective and relevant throughout your retirement journey.

The Mehtas' Smartly Diversified Retirement Plan

Mrs. and Mr. Mehta began planning for retirement in their early 40s with a simple aim: to cover all essential expenses without depending on their children.

They first listed their major needs for old age:

- Housing,
- Daily living,
- Healthcare,
- Transportation,
- And insurance.

With inflation in mind, they realised their future costs could be almost four times today's expenses.

To secure this, they built a diversified retirement portfolio:

- Mutual funds for long-term growth and inflation protection

- PPF and Fixed Deposits for a stable monthly income
- A small rental property to cover housing and utility expenses
- Endowment plans, whose maturity amount was later used to purchase an annuity for guaranteed lifelong income
- Health insurance to prevent medical costs from draining their savings
- And they also created a contingency fund for unexpected expenses

They also followed an income–expense matching strategy, earmarking:

- Rental income for housing,
- FD/PPF returns for groceries and transport,
- And the annuity income for regular fixed costs.

This ensured predictability and peace of mind.

- By the time they retired, the Mehtas had multiple steady income streams, full healthcare protection, and a financial cushion for emergencies.
- Their essential expenses were covered comfortably, allowing them to live with dignity, freedom, and zero dependence on their children.

Retirement planning is not a one-size-fits-all approach.

Understanding the spectrum of available financial instruments allows you to create a retirement plan tailored to your specific needs. A diversified strategy, comprising growth-oriented investments as well as stable income sources like life insurance and annuity schemes, ensures a consistent coverage of essential expenses throughout retirement. By this approach, retirement planning offers not just financial adequacy but also peace of mind in your golden years.

CHAPTER 7

THE PRINCIPLES OF EFFECTIVE RETIREMENT PLANNING

> *"Asset allocation is the compass; diversification is the safety net."*
> ***– Vikas Arora***

In financial parlance, 'diversification' is a mantra often preached and practiced. It pertains to the method of spreading investments across a variety of financial instruments, thereby reducing exposure to any single asset or risk. The underlying principle is simple, but powerful: "Do not put all your eggs in one basket."

Understanding Risk
The Yin and Yang of Investments

Risk and return in investments go hand in hand.

- While mutual funds and stocks have the potential for high returns, they also carry a higher level of risk.
- Conversely, bonds and fixed income securities may offer lower returns but come with less risk.
- Understanding your risk tolerance is crucial in deciding the mix of high-risk and low-risk assets in your portfolio.

Decoding Diversification & Instruments: A Multi-Layered Approach to Retirement Planning

In this chapter, let's look at the various instruments available and their advantages and associated risks, if any, in detail.

1. **Investment Funds**

   - **Mutual Funds: A Pool of Opportunities**

     Mutual funds represent collective investments from numerous individuals, pooled together to invest in a diversified portfolio of stocks, bonds, and other securities. They extend benefits such as professional management, diversification, and liquidity. However, it's essential to note that investments in mutual funds are subject to market risks, and their performance must be reviewed periodically.

   - **Stocks: The Potential Powerhouse of Returns**

     Investing in the equity market, although fraught with risk, presents a substantial potential for high returns. However, the onus lies on making informed choices, considering company performance, industry growth, and market trends. Despite the inherent volatility, equity investments can substantially boost corpus growth for long-term retirement planning. Again, the performance of stocks is subject to market volatility and requires diligent tracking.

   - **Bonds: The Beacon of Stability**

     Bonds, or fixed-income securities, are considered safer than equities and offer stable returns. They pledge to pay a fixed interest amount periodically and return the principal amount on maturity. Government bonds, in particular, are practically risk-free and offer a reliable income stream.

2. **Life Insurance: Protecting Your Financial Future**

   Life insurance is an indispensable component of retirement planning. It delivers financial security to your dependents in the case of unforeseen events.

   Endowment plans, a variant of life insurance, offer the dual benefits of insurance and investment, paying out a lump sum on surviving the policy term.

3. **Annuities: The Promise of Guaranteed Regular Income**

   Annuity schemes stand as contracts that promise a steady income stream post-retirement, in return for a lump-sum investment or a series of payments. They ensure peace of mind by guaranteeing a regular payout to meet essential expenses during retirement.

Creating a Balanced Portfolio: The Art of Diversification in Practice

The creation of a balanced retirement portfolio entails strategically diversifying investments across asset classes.

The goal is to balance risk and returns in line with individual financial goals, risk appetite, and investment horizon, as detailed in the 3 key insights below.

Understanding and Managing Market Volatility: Stay the Course

Equity markets are prone to volatility, which can induce stress and potentially lead to rash investment decisions. It's important to understand that market volatility is a natural part of the investment cycle. Rather than reacting impulsively to market downturns, staying the course and adhering to your long-term investment strategy can lead to better outcomes.

Portfolio Rebalancing: Aligning with Changing Times

Portfolio rebalancing is a critical aspect of retirement planning. As market conditions change, your portfolio's asset allocation may shift from its original design. **Regular rebalancing helps bring your portfolio back into alignment with your desired asset allocation and risk tolerance.**

Discipline and Regular Reviews: The Bedrock of Successful Retirement Planning

Investing necessitates not just a strategic plan, but also the discipline to adhere to it. Regular investment, resisting panic selling during market downturns, and avoiding the chase of short-term trends are essential. Life changes and shifts in economic conditions may call for plan adjustments, reinforcing the importance of regular reviews.

Effective retirement planning, underpinned by the principles of diversification, risk management, and regular portfolio rebalancing, is an ongoing process. A prudent mix of mutual funds, stocks, bonds, life insurance, and annuities can construct a robust retirement plan that withstands time and ensures financial comfort in your golden years. It's highly recommended to invest in instruments that provide lifelong guaranteed and passive income. Therefore, regular discipline and review form the bedrock of successful retirement planning.

CHAPTER 8

RETIREMENT SAVINGS AND INVESTMENT OPTIONS

"Retirement planning is not about choosing the best investment—it's about choosing the right combination that supports the life you want to live."

– Vikas Arora

The Investment Spectrum

Retirement planning introduces you to a wide spectrum of investment options, each with its unique set of benefits, risks, and growth potentials. Navigating this diverse landscape can be daunting. Hence, understanding this spectrum and aligning your investment choices with your retirement goals becomes critical.

A. Traditional Retirement Investment Vehicles: PPF, FDs, and More

Historically, Indians have gravitated towards safer, less risky investment options such as the Public Provident Fund (PPF) and Fixed Deposits (FDs) for retirement planning. Although these investment vehicles offer guaranteed returns, they often yield at a lower rate.

- **Public Provident Fund (PPF): A Long-Term Safe Haven**
  PPF is a long-term investment option that offers attractive interest rates, and the returns are fully exempt from tax. However, the PPF's less liquid nature and its long tenure of 15 years might not align with everyone's financial goals. It's a preferred choice for those who want a risk-free avenue for retirement savings and are ready to lock in funds for a longer duration.
- **Fixed Deposits (FDs): The Time-Tested Investment Vehicle**
  FDs offer stability and guaranteed returns, making them a favorite among conservative investors. However, the downside is that returns from FDs may not outpace inflation significantly, thereby eroding the real rate of return. While it provides a sense of security, the limited growth potential makes FDs less suitable for long-term wealth accumulation.

B. Modern Investment Opportunities: Mutual Funds, Stocks, and Bonds

Today's investor has access to a plethora of investment avenues, offering the potential for higher returns. However, these options often come with higher risks compared to traditional ones.

- **Mutual Funds: A Balanced Approach to Investing**
  Mutual funds provide diversified exposure to equities, bonds, or a mix of both, depending on the type of fund. They enable investors to tap into the growth potential of equities and the stability of bonds, fostering a balanced investment approach.
- **Direct Investment in Stocks and Bonds: Higher Risks, Higher Returns**
  Investing directly in stocks and bonds can lead to higher returns. However, they require significant financial literacy and risk tolerance. It's crucial to research and understand

these markets or hire a financial advisor to navigate these waters effectively.

- **Annuity Schemes and Life Insurance: Guaranteed Returns**

  Annuity schemes promise a guaranteed income stream post-retirement. They act as a safety net, ensuring you have a consistent cash flow during your non-working years. Though annuities might not offer high returns, they do provide a sense of security and stability, crucial for retired individuals.

- **Life Insurance: A Safety Net for Your Loved Ones**

  Life insurance, especially endowment and term plans, serves a dual purpose. They provide a financial safety net to your dependents and also double up as a means of saving that can be inherited by your loved ones.

- **Real Estate: A Tangible Asset with Dual Benefits**

  Real estate has long been a preferred investment option in India, attributable to the dual benefits of potential capital appreciation and rental income. However, it also comes with its set of challenges, including a high initial investment, illiquidity, and susceptibility to market volatilities. Despite the challenges, real estate can form a part of your retirement portfolio, especially if you have a high risk tolerance and a long-term investment horizon.

- **Understanding Gold as an Investment Option**

  Investing in gold has been an age-old tradition in India. Gold is considered a hedge against inflation and a safe haven during economic uncertainties. It can be a part of your retirement portfolio, providing diversification and serving as an inflation hedge. However, the investment should be in moderation as gold doesn't provide regular income or dividends like stocks or bonds.

- **Retirement Funds and Pension Schemes: Tailored for Post-Retirement**

  Retirement funds and pension schemes, specifically designed for providing income post-retirement, are other options to consider. The National Pension Scheme (NPS), Atal Pension Yojana (APY), and Employee Provident Fund (EPF) are some of the popular retirement-focused schemes in India. They offer tax benefits and can provide a substantial corpus at the time of retirement.

Balancing Act: How Mr. Gupta Secured His Tomorrow

Mr. Gupta, a 35-year-old software professional, wanted stability without sacrificing growth. Recognising that no single investment could meet all future needs, he built a layered, diversified portfolio:

- **Safety & Stability:** He invested in **PPF and FDs** to create a low-risk base for essential expenses.
- **Growth & Wealth Building:** A mix of **equity mutual funds and select stocks** provided long-term growth, helping him beat inflation. He complemented this with corporate and government bonds for steady interest income.
- **Tangible Assets & Inflation Hedge:** Mr. Gupta purchased a **small rental property** that generates monthly rental income and offers long-term capital appreciation. He also allocates a **small portion to gold** for its historical value as a crisis hedge.
- **Security & Income Assurance:** To safeguard his family and create future income stability, he holds **life insurance**, an **endowment policy**, and a **deferred annuity plan** that will activate post-retirement.

The Outcome

Mr. Gupta's portfolio now stands on three strong pillars:

- Protection (PPF, insurance, annuity)
- Growth (mutual funds, equities)
- Stability (FDs, bonds, real estate, gold)

This blend gives him inflation-beating returns, monthly income potential, risk mitigation, and long-term security, all essential for a robust retirement plan.

Choosing the Right Mix

Selecting the right mix of retirement savings and investment options is a delicate balancing act between risk and return, liquidity and growth, and present and future needs. It requires understanding various investment avenues and aligning them with one's financial goals, risk appetite, and investment horizon.

Diversification: Spreading the Risk

Building a diversified portfolio can help mitigate risk. Rather than putting all your money into one type of investment, spreading your investments across different asset classes can help cushion against market downturns.

Regular Review and Rebalancing: Staying on Track

Investments should be regularly reviewed and rebalanced to ensure they are in line with your changing life circumstances and market conditions. This proactive approach helps in keeping your retirement planning on track.

Start Early, Invest Wisely: The Key to Successful Retirement Planning

The retirement planning journey is unique for each individual, reflecting their specific circumstances, goals, and preferences. Starting early, investing wisely, and reviewing the plan periodically is the recipe for a successful retirement plan. Remember, the most important thing about retirement planning is not just about building a large corpus but ensuring a steady stream of income to maintain your lifestyle in the golden years.

CHAPTER 9

HEALTHCARE AND RETIREMENT

"Health may decline with age, but your
financial peace shouldn't.
Plan early, protect deeply.
The real cost of ageing is not time,
it's unplanned healthcare."
– Vikas Arora

In the golden years of life, maintaining health becomes a significant concern. The ageing process makes our bodies more susceptible to illness, demanding increased medical attention. In a country like India, where the healthcare cost trajectory is steadily ascending, these expenses become a key element in retirement planning. In particular, chronic illnesses can result in hospital bills skyrocketing to over 50 lakhs, posing a potential risk to drain your hard-earned savings within minutes.

Health Insurance: Your Safety Net Against Medical Expenses

Today, health insurance is not a luxury but an essential shield against mounting medical costs. It acts as a bulwark, protecting your retirement savings from being consumed by unforeseen medical emergencies.

Having a comprehensive health insurance plan is crucial.

Such a plan would cover various medical needs, including:

- Regular health check-ups
- Medication
- Hospitalization
- And even special coverage for critical illnesses.

The Huge Cost of Not Planning for Health Care

Take the case of Mr. Singh, who had meticulously saved for his retirement.

However, he had overlooked the importance of health insurance.

At the age of 66, he was diagnosed with a heart condition that required immediate surgery and long-term care.

The cost of treatment, medications, and rehabilitation care quickly **mounted to 40 lakhs, eating into a substantial portion of his retirement savings.**

This example underscores the importance of having a robust health insurance policy in place.

Planning for Long-term Care Expenses

Long-term care, an often-ignored aspect of retirement planning, caters to individuals with chronic illnesses or disabilities.

Such care includes:

- services like in-home care,
- community programs,
- or assisted living facilities.

These services tend to be expensive and could extend over many years, making it crucial to consider them in your retirement planning.

Looking Beyond Immediate Medical Expenses: The Cost of Long-Term Care

Consider this: you or your spouse might require long-term care such as a nursing home or in-home nursing assistance.

The cost of such care can be astronomical, and it is often not fully covered by regular health insurance.

A study shows that in India, **the average cost of a private room in a nursing home is around INR 30,000 per month** (as of 2023), and this cost is expected to rise in the future.

Healthcare Savings Accounts: A Tool for Future Healthcare Expenses

- Healthcare savings accounts, like medical savings accounts or health savings accounts, provide another pathway to fund healthcare costs.
- These accounts are specifically designed to accumulate funds for future healthcare expenses.
- They offer certain tax benefits, making them a valuable instrument in a retiree's financial kit.
- Regular contributions to such an account, combined with the tax benefits, could build a considerable corpus over time to cover health-related expenses during retirement.

The Role of Emergency Funds in Healthcare Planning

In addition to healthcare savings accounts, having an emergency fund is crucial for handling unexpected healthcare costs. An emergency fund is a cash reserve that you set aside to cover unexpected expenses, such as medical emergencies, without needing to tap into your retirement savings or take on debt. A good rule of thumb is to have enough money in your emergency fund to cover at least three to six months' worth of living expenses.

Fighting Cancer with Strength & Financial Security

While she was in her early forties, Mrs. Bajaj, a schoolteacher, had understood one truth early:

Retirement is peaceful only when healthcare is planned well. Having seen her mother struggle with medical bills, she decided her retirement strategy would place **health first, wealth second,** because one directly protects the other.

Her Strategy

- She purchased a comprehensive ₹25 lakh health insurance policy with critical illness add-ons for cancer, cardiac issues, and organ failure.
- She opened a Health Savings Account, contributing a small amount every month for routine check-ups, medicines, and future medical needs.
- She maintained a 6-month emergency fund, strictly for unforeseen healthcare expenses.
- She also explored long-term care planning, ensuring she could afford home nursing if needed.

The Turning Point

- At 64, Mrs. Bajaj was diagnosed with an early-stage cancer. Her treatment cost ₹18 lakhs.
- Health insurance covered hospitalization, surgery, and chemo.
- Her health savings account helped pay for follow-up scans and medicines.
- Her emergency fund covered additional supportive care without disturbing her investments or pension.

The Outcome

- Because of her preparation:
- Her retirement corpus remained untouched.
- She avoided debt, stress, or liquidation of assets.
- She continued her retirement life exactly as planned, with dignity, independence, and peace.

Lesson

- Healthcare planning is not optional; it is the backbone of a secure retirement.
- Mrs. Bajaj's example proves that when health emergencies arrive, financial preparedness decides whether retirement stays peaceful or becomes fragile.

The Intersection of Healthcare and Wealth

The realms of healthcare and retirement are intrinsically intertwined. Absent adequate planning, escalating healthcare costs can swiftly drain retirement savings. To safeguard your health and wealth simultaneously, incorporating health insurance, planning for long-term care, and a healthcare savings account should be essential elements of your retirement strategy. The secret lies in starting to plan early and conducting regular reviews to stay abreast of the increasing healthcare costs.

With advancements in medical technology, the nature and cost of healthcare are continually evolving. It is important to keep abreast of these changes and regularly revisit your healthcare financial strategy. This way, you can ensure you're adequately covered and can adjust your savings plan to meet the potential rise in healthcare costs in the future. This forward-thinking approach is the cornerstone of an effective retirement plan.

CHAPTER 10

ESTATE PLANNING AND LEGACY

> *"Wealth can build empires or break families. Legacy planning is the art of ensuring it does the former without sacrificing your own freedom."*
>
> **– *Vikas Arora***

"Your legacy is not just what you leave for others. It is also what you preserve for yourself while you are still here."

Legacy planning is a meticulous process, much like crafting the final act of your life's financial story. It requires careful thought, balanced decisions, and a clear understanding of both your future and the future of those you wish to provide for. Many individuals approach legacy building by accumulating real estate or large assets, driven by the belief that wealth passed down in material form defines a strong inheritance.

For instance, **Bollywood's *"Baazaar"*** captures this mindset well, showing how the relentless pursuit of wealth can overshadow ethics, relationships, and peace of mind. In real life, too, aggressive accumulation can become a double-edged sword. Excessive property ownership often leads to complicated legal battles and emotional friction among family members, resembling the conflicts portrayed in **"*Waqt:* The Race Against Time,"** where misunderstood financial intentions create deep familial rifts.

The first principle of legacy planning is simple yet often forgotten: secure your own retirement before planning what to leave behind.

When individuals compromise their retirement comfort in the name of creating a larger inheritance, they risk spending their later years in financial stress or dependency.

A legacy should never come at the cost of your own dignity or stability.

Instead of tying up money in illiquid assets like multiple properties, a well-balanced portfolio that includes life insurance endowment plans, annuities, pension schemes, and diversified financial investments creates a strong base. This allows you to maintain independence while still preparing meaningful assets for your heirs. A diversified approach also reduces the burden of property-related disputes, avoids emotional strain on children, and ensures your retirement remains peaceful.

When Life Throws Curve Balls

Planning your legacy also means preparing for the twists life may unexpectedly bring. Illness, emergencies, financial shocks, and changing family circumstances can influence how your assets should be managed. If a sudden health condition requires long-term care, liquid and predictable income becomes essential. If an unforeseen expense arises, depending solely on real estate can leave you financially trapped. By maintaining a mix of predictable income sources, emergency reserves, and clear asset structures, you protect both your present and the assets you wish to pass down.

Unexpected events can also reshape how your estate is eventually distributed.

This is why legal clarity is a critical part of legacy planning.

- A well-drafted will, updated nominations on all investments, and properly documented ownership reduce complications for your heirs.
- Without these precautions, even the simplest estates can become entangled in delays or conflicts.
- Similarly, appointing trusted individuals through powers of attorney.
- And documenting your healthcare wishes ensures that your voice is respected if you are unable to make decisions yourself.
- These steps safeguard your estate against confusion and protect your family from avoidable stress.

A meaningful legacy extends beyond material possessions. Many retirees choose to pass on values, wisdom, and emotional security by funding education for grandchildren, supporting charitable causes, or gifting structured financial tools like annuities and insurance plans that promote financial discipline for the next generation. These thoughtful choices often have a deeper and more lasting impact than property alone.

To illustrate the contrast, consider two families.

The Khannas Vs The Kaushiks: Prudence Wins

The Khannas spent years accumulating multiple properties to leave behind.

- When the time came to distribute them, each child wanted a different share based on emotional attachments.
- Arguments escalated, legal notices followed, and the parents spent their final years mediating disputes rather than enjoying peace.

In contrast, the Kaushiks focused on securing their own retirement with annuities, insurance, and investments.

- They kept only one primary home and distributed their financial assets clearly through a legally documented will.
- Their children inherited smoothly, and the family bond remained intact.

The difference lay in clarity, simplicity, and balance.

Legacy planning is not only for the wealthy. It is for anyone who wants to ensure family harmony, financial clarity, and personal independence in their later years. It helps you transfer your assets smoothly, prevents conflict, and ensures that your retirement remains secure. Ultimately, true legacy is not about the size of what you leave behind, but the peace, clarity, and love with which you leave it.

CHAPTER 11

STEPPING INTO TOMORROW

THE CONFIDENCE OF A WELL-PLANNED RETIREMENT

> *"Retirement is not the end of your story; it is the beginning of a chapter you finally get to write on your own terms."*
> ***– Vikas Arora***

Retirement is not a number, not an age, and not a bank balance. It is a vision. It is the freedom to live life on your terms without fear or dependence. As you have seen throughout this book, retirement planning is not a single decision but a series of simple steps repeated consistently over time. Small choices made early create comfort, dignity, and peace in your later years. When you save regularly, invest wisely, and protect yourself with insurance and healthcare planning, you build a safety net that supports you through every season of life. When you diversify, review your progress, and stay disciplined, your money grows steadily and silently. When you secure your retirement first and plan your legacy with clarity, you protect not only your wealth but also your family's harmony. This journey is not about predicting the future but preparing for it. The tools you have learned, from mutual funds and annuities to health insurance and estate planning, all serve one purpose: to put you in control. Retirement is a time to rediscover yourself. It is when you can follow dreams paused for decades, spend unhurried moments with loved ones, explore new passions, and live with peace in your heart. The goal of everything you have learned is simple. To help you create a life where money supports you quietly in the background while you live boldly in the foreground.

- Start early if you can.
- Start today if you haven't.
- The best time to build your retirement was yesterday. The second-best time is now.
- Your journey to financial independence and a joyful retirement begins with your next step.

Take it with confidence. Your future is waiting.

BONUS CHAPTER

NEW AGE RETIREMENT STRATEGIES FOR A CHANGING INDIA

Retirement planning in India is evolving faster than ever. Longer life spans, digital tools, new financial products, and changing family structures have transformed how today's retirees must plan their futures. The old approach of relying only on pensions, children, or property is slowly fading. Today's retirees need smarter income strategies, better healthcare planning, emotional preparedness, and tools that match the demands of modern life. This chapter highlights some of the most important new-age retirement concepts every future retiree in India should understand and incorporate.

1. **The Rise of Longevity Planning**

   Indians are living well into their eighties, and many into their nineties. This means retirement may last 30 to 40 years. Longevity planning focuses on creating income that lasts for decades, not just years. It involves designing multiple income layers, delaying annuity purchases for higher payouts, preparing for rising healthcare needs, and adjusting spending patterns across early, mid, and late retirement phases.

2. **The Bucket Strategy for Retirement Income**

   A rising trend globally and increasingly adopted in India. Retirement savings are divided into three buckets based on time horizons. Bucket one holds very safe instruments like FDs or liquid funds for the next one to three years. Bucket two holds medium-term investments such as short-duration debt funds for years three to ten. Bucket three holds long-term instruments, including equity, for ten years and beyond. This method protects retirees from short-term market volatility while allowing long-term growth.

3. **The Rise of Senior Living Communities**

   Modern senior living communities are no longer seen as a compromise. They offer medical support, safety, social activities, fitness, hobby centres, and like-minded companionship. Many retirees are choosing these communities early to enjoy independence without burdening their children. In cities like Pune, Bangalore, Coimbatore, and Gurgaon, this trend is becoming mainstream.

4. **Digital Wills and Online Estate Tools**

   India has seen a surge in platforms that let individuals create digital wills, store important documents, track nominations, and keep estate information accessible and updated. This eliminates the risk of missing documents or unclaimed investments. Digital tools ensure heirs receive what is intended without confusion.

5. **Long-Term Care Insurance and Senior Care Riders**

   With rising cases of Alzheimer's, dementia, and age related disabilities, insurers now offer riders that cover long-term care, in-home assistance, and assisted living expenses. These products help retirees avoid sudden financial depletion during chronic illness and protect family members from emotional and financial strain.

6. **Retirement Coaching and Emotional Readiness**

   A new trend is emerging in India. Retirement coaching focuses on helping navigate identity shifts, purpose and mental health, building routines, combating loneliness, and reshaping daily life after leaving work.

Financial stability alone does not guarantee a fulfilling retirement; emotional readiness is equally important. Many new retirees benefit from coaching sessions that help them transition smoothly into this new chapter.

7. **The SIP to SWP Blueprint**

   One of the most powerful modern approaches. During working years, individuals grow wealth through SIPs (Systemic Investment Plans) in mutual funds. At retirement, these investments seamlessly shift to SWPs (Systemic Withdrawal Plans), offering predictable monthly payouts. This creates a self-driven pension that adjusts for inflation and continues generating returns.

Financial Security Overcomes Physical Mobility

The Sahnis, both government employees, assumed their pension would be enough. But their financial planner introduced longevity planning. They added an annuity, created a bucket strategy to manage income for the next twenty years, and purchased long-term care insurance. When Mrs Sahni developed mobility challenges at 72, their rider covered her in-home rehabilitation and equipment. Their retirement remained financially comfortable because they planned for a longer life instead of assuming a shorter one.

How The Bucket Strategy Saved The Shettys' Retirement

The Shettys retired in 2020, just before the pandemic market crash.

Because their planner had divided their money into buckets, their short-term funds were untouched by market volatility. They had three years of income safely set aside, while the long-term bucket recovered over time.

Without this approach, they might have withdrawn money in a downturn and permanently damaged their retirement corpus.

The world of retirement is changing, and your planning must evolve with it. Today's retirees need to prepare not just financially but medically, emotionally, and digitally. By embracing new concepts like longevity planning, bucket strategies, digital wills, senior living options, and structured investment-to-income transitions, you give yourself the confidence to step into retirement with clarity and security. These tools empower you to live longer, healthier, calmer, and financially independent lives.